Hidden in Their Hearts

by

Valerie Masin

Illustrations by Rachel Masin

WestBow
PRESS
A DIVISION OF THOMAS NELSON

ISBN: 978-1-4497-1877-0 (sc)
ISBN: 978-1-4497-1878-7 (e)

Library of Congress Control Number: 2011930942

WestBow Press books may be ordered through booksellers or by contacting:

WestBow Press
A Division of Thomas Nelson
1663 Liberty Drive
Bloomington, IN 47403
www.westbowpress.com
1-(866) 928-1240

Printed in the United States of America

WestBow Press rev. date: 6/17/2011

to James, Richele, and Hannah
for teaching me that little ones can learn and
understand the deep things of God

Introduction:

Welcome to *Hidden in Their Hearts* the activity book designed to show that there is a way to help three to seven year old children memorize Scripture and apply God's word to their lives while having fun at the same time. This book will help you capitalize on the children's eagerness and willingness to learn and assist you in teaching them to hide God's Word in their hearts. Enjoy the unique opportunity you have to help these little ones increase in their knowledge and love of their Lord Jesus Christ. It will be time well spent.

General Instructions:

Hidden In Their Hearts is a very versatile resource book. Pages can be used in any order you choose. It can be used in a classroom setting or one-on-one between parent and child. The activities in this book are simple and can be done with minimal preparation. There is an adult page to go with each verse children are to learn followed by a student page which will engage children in memorizing the verse. Each adult page contains a talk about section to help you focus the conversation about the verse, instructions for how to complete the student page, and an additional activities section to help you expand the topic if you desire. Suggested teacher or parent questions and comments are in bold print with student responses following in parenthesis. You are definitely encouraged to say the verse with the children several times during each learning session.

If desired, you can assemble each of the memory verse pages into a book for each child. You could also make an extra page for the class and make a class book sending the individual pages home. Each time you add a new page, be sure to read the whole book or at least several pages as the book gets longer. The repetition will help children hide God's word in their hearts. If you choose to send each individual page home, encourage parents to put the pages into a binder so they can read at home!

Depending on the age of the children you are working with, they may or may not be able to respond to the talk about questions the first time you ask them. Remember, this is a learning process, so it is acceptable to talk about the answer with them.

Additional materials you may find helpful to have on hand:

1. Pictures or stickers of Jesus, the Bible or the world
2. Magazines
3. Individual pictures of the children participating in the book activities (optional)
4. *Little Ones Sing Praise Songbook* (LOSP) Concordia Publishing House (optional)
5. Various Art Supplies

All Bible verses are taken from New International Version.

As you begin, it is my prayer that God will richly bless you and the children you teach. May you all come to stand in awe of our living Savior.

Colossians 3:16:

Let the word of Christ dwell in you richly.

To talk about: What is the Word of Christ?(Bible) Show children a Bible . **In the Bible, God tells us how much He loves us. He tells us more about Him, and He tells us how to serve Him. There are many important things to learn from the Bible. We will learn from the Bible our whole lives. The verse says to let the word dwell in us. What does dwell mean?**(live in) **Can you tell me where you dwell? How can we let God's Word dwell or live in us?** (We can learn Bible verses. We can think about God and His Word in all that we say and do.) **When we think of someone who is rich, what do we think of?** (someone who has lots of money) **What do you think it means to let God's word dwell in us richly? Should we read the Bible just a little and put it away and forget about it?** (no) **We need to really study the Bible and learn more and more about God. Where are some places you can think about God?** (any answer the children give will be acceptable) **What are some things you can remember about God?** (Always with us, forgives us, loves us)

Instructions: Children should decorate the person on the student page to look like themselves. Using a permanent marker, help the children to draw a Bible on the inside of the body or place a sticker of the Bible in the center. **Why did we put a Bible inside the person?** (help us to remember God's Word is to live or dwell in us)

Additional activities:

- Sing "B-I-B-L-E"(LOSP 48)
- Make a Bible Badge to wear today. Cut a circle out of construction paper and put a Bible sticker in the circle. Have children repeat the Bible words as you attach the badge to them. Say: **"Whenever you see the badge remember our Bible words and remember how much God loves and cares for you."**

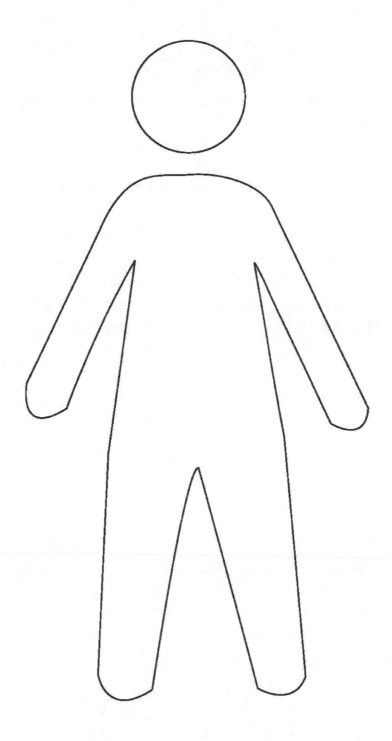

Let the word of Christ dwell in you richly.

Colossians 3:16

Psalm 27:6b

I will sing and make music to the Lord.

To talk about: Do you like to sing? How are some ways that people make music? (play instruments) Let children pantomime the playing of different instruments. **We can also make music by clapping our hands, stomping our feet and whistling. There are lots of ways to make music to the Lord. Who is the Lord?** (God) **Why would we want to sing and make music to the Lord?** (We want to praise and thank Him. We are happy about all that He has done for us. We love Him.) **Why do we want to praise and thank God or the Lord?** (He sent Jesus to be our Savior. He forgives our sins. He loves and takes care of us. He is always with us. He is our best friend)

Instructions: Have children draw a picture of themselves singing on the student page. Show children how to draw an open mouth on their person so it looks like someone singing. Find pictures of musical instruments and let children paste them around the page.

Additional activities:

- Make and decorate simple musical instruments. One example is to make shakers from paper plates. Let children decorate two paper plates. Staple the plates together leaving a small opening for children to place a few dried beans inside. Finish stapling. You could also make drums from oatmeal boxes. Let children decorate a piece of construction paper and then wrap around the container and attach with glue. When instruments are finished, sing your favorite praise songs and have a parade.
- Get out any instruments you have and let children experiment with what kind of music they can make to the Lord.

I will sing and make music to the Lord

Psalm 27:6b

Psalm 23:1
The Lord is my shepherd, I shall not be in want.

To talk about: Have you ever seen a shepherd? If possible show children a picture of a shepherd. **Do you know what a shepherd does?** (takes care of sheep) **What would he have to do to take care of them?** (make sure they have food and water, lead and guide them to keep them safe) **In this verse Jesus is compared to a shepherd. We say the Lord is my shepherd. Who is your good shepherd?** (Jesus) **Remember that a shepherd takes care of his sheep. Why do we say Jesus is our good shepherd?** (He takes care of us.) **How does He take care of you?** (gives food, water, shelter, keeps us safe, leads and guides us and forgives our sins) **We are happy that Jesus is our good shepherd. We are happy to be His sheep.**

Instructions: Hold the student page up for the class. **Who is on our paper?** (Jesus) **What does He have around Him?** (sheep) **Who are the sheep that Jesus takes care of?** (us) **What does Jesus have in His hand?** (a staff) **Notice the shepherd's staff has a hook on the end. The hook is so that a shepherd can reach the sheep if it falls in a deep hole. He can rescue his sheep. Jesus rescued us too. Do you know how He did that?** (He died on the cross) **What did He rescue us from when He died on the cross for us?** (sin, death and the devil) Have children color the picture of Jesus as a shepherd. Paste a picture of the child on the picture of the sheep or have them draw a picture of themselves on the sheep.

Additional activities:

- Sing: "I am Jesus Little Lamb".
- Have children pretend to be sheep. Lead or guide them to green pastures and quiet water. Protect them from wild animals. Bring them in the sheepfold for the night calling each child by name. Lay down in the gate to protect your sheep. Compare the shepherd to Jesus. **What happens when the sheep are not close to the shepherd?** (could get hurt or lost) **Who should we stay close to?** (Jesus)
- Have children glue cotton balls on a picture of a sheep . Write or have children write "The Lord is my shepherd."

**The Lord is my shepherd I
shall not be in want.**

Psalm 23:1

Genesis 1:1

In the beginning God created the
heavens and the earth.

To talk about: What does the word create mean? (to make) **Can you think of something you have created?** (drawings, buildings with blocks, and animals from play dough) **Is it hard to create something? Do you know who created the earth?** (God) **Yes, God created everything we see around us in nature. Before God made the world there was nothing but darkness and then God spoke and everything appeared.** This could be demonstrated by shutting off the lights and saying, "let there be light," and turning on the switch or having various pictures of things God created and saying, "God said let there be...." **Isn't God amazing to be able to make everything just by speaking? Sometimes when we make things we are not very happy with them. We just want to start over. God made everything perfect the first time. He looked at everything He created and said, "It is good." Do you know what we mean when we say God created the heavens?** (He made the sun, moon, stars, planets, comets, and everything in the sky.) **What does it mean God created the earth?** (He made our world and everything in it.)

Instructions: Using a blue crayon have children color the top portion of the student page. Children could also add star stickers or draw a sun in the heavens. Tell them the blue color and stickers, if added, represent the heavens God made. Have them add a sticker of the world in the second space on the page. Remind students that this is a picture of the earth and that God made everything on the earth as well as in the heavens.

Additional Activities:

- Sing any song about creation like "Who Can Make a Flower".
- Read the creation account from a children's Bible.
- Weather permitting take a nature walk to see the wonderful things God created. Give children a small bag so they can collect interesting things along the way. Let children glue magazine pictures and things found on the nature walk to construction paper and make a poster. Write "Look What God Created" at the top. This could be an individual or a class project.

In the beginning God created

the heavens and the earth.

Genesis 1:1

Ephesians 6:1

Children obey your parents in the Lord for this is right.

To talk about: Who is this verse talking to? (children) **Are you a child?** (Yes) **This verse is talking to you. Who are your parents? What does it mean to obey?** (to do what you are told) **What does God tell us He wants us to do in this passage?** (obey our parents) **Why is it important to obey?** (God tells us to, and it helps keep us safe.) **Your parents know many more things than you do. God has given them the job to love you and keep you safe. When you disobey, you might get hurt. It is your parents' job to raise you according to God's will. What is your job?** (to obey) **Why did God give you parents or other caregivers?** (He loves us) **How else does God show His love for you?** (He sent Jesus to die for us, forgives us, takes care of us) **One of the biggest ways God takes care of you is by giving you parents to love and care for you. Who else besides parents should you obey?** (teachers, grandparents, babysitters) **God gives you all these people because He loves you. You show you love them and God when you obey without arguing.**

Instructions: Have children place a photo of themselves and their siblings, if desired, above the word children on the student page. Place a picture of their parents in the next opening on the page. If actual pictures are unavailable, allow children to draw pictures of themselves and their parents.

Additional Activity:

- Play a game of Simon Says with one simple change. When you give the directions, say "Mommy, Daddy, or Teacher says." Encourage your children in their obeying.

Children

**obey your parents in the
Lord for this is right.**

Ephesians 6:1

1 John 4:19:

We love because He first loved us.

To talk about: Do you know who the He in the verse is talking about? (God) **How did God love us first?** (He sent Jesus to be our Savior. He forgives all our sins. He made us.) **God's love is perfect. He gives us the example of how to love. He also helps us learn how to love others. He wants us to show other people His love and He helps us do that. Who can we love now that we know how much God loves us?** (God and other people) **How do we show our love for God?** (pray, sing, read the Bible, go to church and Sunday School, love other people) **How do we show other people we love them?** (obey parents, help with chores, share our toys, invite someone to Sunday School, send someone a card or a picture, pray for them.)

Instructions: I'm going to give you a big heart. What do hearts remind us of? (love) Have children glue the heart in the center of the student page. **Next, we're going to put a sticker of Jesus in the center of the heart. What will that help us remember?** (Jesus loves us) **Jesus love is great big. He loves everyone perfectly.** Place a picture of the child as well as pictures of people cut from magazines or family photos around the outside of the heart. Have children draw arrows from Jesus to the people. **We draw the arrows from Jesus to the people to show Jesus loved us first.** Draw arrows from the people to other people. **These arrows show that with Jesus help and because He loved us first we can love others.**

Additional Activities:

- Sing "Oh How I Love Jesus" (LOSP 44) and "We Love" (LOSP 54)
- Make a poster. Divide the paper in half. On one side write Love God. On the other side write Love Others. Look in magazines or old Sunday School leaflets to find pictures of people loving God or others. Older children may want to draw their own pictures. For the very young, you may want to have the pictures found and let children decide which side of the poster to put them on.

We love because He first loved us.

1 John 4:19

Hebrews 13:8

Jesus Christ is the same yesterday and today and forever.

To talk about: Bring out a calendar and talk about the terms yesterday, today, tomorrow and forever. **Everyday in our lives things change. We grow, we eat at a different time, we go someplace different. Things are always changing. Our Bible words tell us that Jesus never changes. We can count on Him to always be the same loving and forgiving God all throughout our lives. No matter what changes happen to us, Jesus will stay the same in our lives. He always loves us and always will love us. He loves our parents and grandparents and great grandparents and has loved them since they were little. He will keep loving them. He will keep loving you too even as you get bigger. You can never get too big for God to love you. Someday when you are mommies and daddies He will love your children. He always keeps His promises to forgive us, love us, care for us, and be with us. Do you know who the first people on earth were?** (Adam and Eve) **God even loved Adam and Eve the same way He loves us and He will love the last people to live on earth the same way He does us. Our God is amazing!**

Instructions: Have children draw three boxes on the student page and then put three identical stickers of Jesus in the boxes. **What can you tell me about these stickers of Jesus?** (They are all the same.) **These pictures of Jesus that are all the same will remind us that Jesus never changes. He is the same yesterday, today and forever.**

Additional activity:

- Divide a piece of paper into two sections. Paste a picture of a baby, a child and an adult in one section. If you are doing this with your own children, have them paste a picture of themselves as a baby and a picture of them now on the paper. Write, "People keep growing and changing" under the pictures. Place a picture of Jesus in the other section. Write, "Jesus never changes" under His picture.

Jesus Christ is the same yesterday and today and forever.

Hebrews 13:8

Acts 1:8

You will be my witnesses...to the ends of the earth.

To talk about: What does it mean to be a witness? (Tell about what you have seen or heard and know to be true) **Right now you are witnessing me talking to you. When you tell someone else what I have said you are also witnessing. What are some things Jesus wants us to tell others about Him?** (He loves them. He forgives them. He is always there. He takes care of them.) **How else can we witness besides using our mouths to talk to people?** (show people kindness, do the things Jesus wants us to because people are watching us.) **Jesus wants us to witness to the ends of the earth. What does that mean?** (He wants us to tell everyone we see about Him and spread the good news that Jesus loves everyone) **He wants everyone in the whole world to know about Him. How can we help the people who are far away telling others about Jesus in different countries?** (We can give our offerings to help them. We can pray for them.) **Even if we can't travel far away to another country, we can still help spread the good news to the ends of the earth through our prayers and offerings.**

Instructions: Have children color the big picture of the world on the student page and put a picture of themselves in the center. **What does Jesus tell us in our verse?** (That we will be His witnesses to the ends of the earth.) Have children draw arrows from themselves to all different parts of the world. **These arrows show that you are telling the whole world? Who are we to tell the whole world about?** (Jesus) **Let's put a sticker of Jesus at the top of our page so we can remember to tell everyone we know about Jesus.**

Additional activity:

- Sing "Go Tell" (LOSP 104)
- Let the children role play how they can be witnesses to the people around them. Examples include: Invite someone to Sunday School, play nicely with other children, take a card to someone who is sick, sing a song for an older person they know, tell someone "Jesus Loves You."
- Visit an assisted living facility or nursing home. Have children sing some songs they know about Jesus and then shake the residents' hands. Before you go or when you get back talk about how you were witnesses for Jesus.

**You will be my witnesses...
to the ends of the earth.**

Acts 1:8

Philippians 4:19a

God will meet all your needs.

To talk about: This verse tells us God will meet all our needs. Needs are the things we need in order to live. Have children make a list of needs and talk about why each is important. Include food, water, shelter, clothes, air, and love. Sample discussion: **Why do we need food?** (to eat) **Food helps to keep us healthy and gives us nutrients to help us grow big and strong.** Continue in this way until you have discussed each of our basic needs. **We have all our needs met because God gives us everything we have. God has also taken care of our biggest need which is our need for a Savior. Who is our Savior?** (Jesus) **What did He do for us?** (died on the cross to take away all our sins) **Why is it so important that God sent His only son Jesus to be our Savior?** (without Him we would be punished by God for our sins)

Instructions: Cut pictures out of magazines and/or draw pictures to represent all our basic needs; food, water, shelter, clothes, love, air and Jesus. Paste the pictures on the student page and label the pictures. Repeat the Bible words.

Additional activity:

- Play a guessing game where you give a clue and children guess which need you are referring to. You could also have children point to the picture on their page so they can all participate. Here are a few suggestions to get you started. Forgives all your sins (Jesus) You need it to breathe (air) You live in it (house) Parents and Jesus give this to you (love) You take a bath in it (water) Continue as long as interest allows. Say a prayer thanking God for meeting all your needs. Have each child say one line. Thank you God for water. Etc.

God will meet all your needs.
Philippians 4:19a

Psalm 119:105:

Your word is a lamp to my feet and a light for my path.

To talk about: What does Your word mean? (God's word, the Bible) **What does a lamp or light do?** (makes things bright) Demonstrate this by taking the children into a dark room and then turning on a light. **This verse compares God's Word, the Bible, to a lamp and a light. How is God's Word like a lamp?** (Brightens our life by helping us. It shows us which way to go. It helps us to make good choices and please God. It tells us about Jesus who died and rose again to forgive us.) **When we believe in Jesus, God's Word will shine like a light for us throughout our life on earth and all the way to heaven.**

Instructions: Children place a sticker of the Bible over the words your word on the student page. **Remember your word is talking about God's word the Bible. Look at the picture with the lamp. What does it look like the lamp may be sitting on?** (a sidewalk) **Do we walk on sidewalks with our feet? Let's draw two little feet on the sidewalk to help us remember that God's Word is a lamp to our feet.** Demonstrate to children how to draw a foot. In the last section have children draw a path. **Do you know what a path is?** (a road) **Our lives are like a road. The road will one day lead us to heaven.** Children color the path yellow to represent light.

Additional activity:

- Set up some different paths to follow in your classroom or in your house. Put blankets or pillows on the floor or arrange chairs to make a path. Add some forks to the path showing you could go in two different directions. Walk down the path with the children. Be sure to carry your Bible with you. When you come to the forks explain, "This path is fighting with my sister. This one is playing nicely with her. God's Word says, 'Love one another'." Repeat the Bible verse before answering each question. "Which way do we go? This path is stay home on Sunday morning and play. This path is go to church and Sunday School. The Bible says, 'Worship the Lord Your God.' Which way do we go? My friend is sick. This path is go and play. This path is stop and pray. The Bible says, 'Pray on all occasions.' Which way do we go?" These of course are only examples. Use situations that are currently relevant to the children you are working with.

Your word

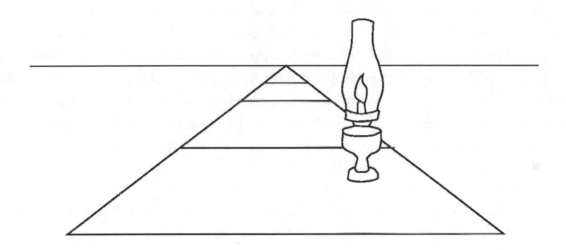

is a lamp to my feet

and a light for my path.

Psalm 119:105

John 3:16:

For God so loved the world that He gave His one and only Son, that whoever believes in Him shall not perish but have eternal life.

To talk about: Where do you live? God sees you and me even though the world is big. He loves every person in the whole world. He loved us so much that He sent His one and only Son, Jesus, to Earth to help us. What did Jesus do for us? (died on the cross to take away our sin.) **What is sin?** (Sin is the bad things we do, say, or think) **Do you believe that Jesus loved you so much that He died on the cross to take away all your sins?** (yes) **Our verse says that if you believe in Jesus you will have eternal life. Do you know what eternal life is?** (living forever with Jesus in heaven) **How will we feel in heaven.** (happy) **God tells us in the Bible that heaven is going to be a wonderful and beautiful place. There will be no more crying or fighting and no one will ever get sick again.**

Instructions: At the top of the student page, have children attach a sticker of the world. **What does it say in this verse that God loved?** (the world) Have children attach a sticker of Jesus and draw a cross in the next section. **Who did God send to earth for us?** (His one and only Son, Jesus) In the third section, give children faces you have cut out of magazines and glue them to the paper. If you are doing this project with your own child, another option would be to find pictures of people your child knows who love Jesus and glue their faces to the paper. **We know that God loves all people and helps them to believe in Him. Everyone who believes in Jesus will be saved. Earlier I asked you if you believed in Jesus and you said yes. Let's make sure to put a picture of you on this paper too.** For the last section, show children how to draw a cloud and to make yellow and orange lines coming out of the cloud to represent God's glory and happiness. **What does God promise all who believe in Him?** (eternal life)

Additional activities:
- Look at a globe. Find where you live. Talk about people living all over the world and that Jesus loves and died for everyone. You could have a little person that you can move around and tape to different parts of the globe. Ask the children: **"Do people live in Africa? Does Jesus love the people who live in Africa?** Continue as time and interest allow.
- Sing: "Jesus Loves Me" (LOSP 42) and "Jesus Loves the Little Children" (LOSP 94)

For God so loved the world

He gave His one and only Son

that whoever believes in Him

shall not perish but have eternal life.

John 3:16

Psalm 119:11a:

I have hidden Your Word in my heart.

To talk about: What does it mean to hide something? (Put it in a place where people can't see it) **If you hide something, do you still know where it is?** (Yes) Demonstrate this by showing children a small item you plan to hide. Ask children to close their eyes. Hide the object. **Do you see where I put the object? You can't see it, but I know right where it is.** Go and get the object. **In this verse what does God tell us to hide?** (His Word) **What does your word mean?** (God's word, the Bible) **The Bible is a very special book. It is God speaking to us. Why do we read the Bible?** (We read to learn about how much Jesus loves us, that He died for us and came back to life,and that He forgives all our sins. We also read to know how Jesus wants us to live) **Where are we supposed to hide God's Word?** (in our heart) **How can we hide God's word in our hearts?** (We learn it like we are doing now) **Why is it important to hide God's word in our hearts?** (God's words will always be with us and no one will ever be able to take it away from us.) **We will always know where to find God's Word. Knowing God's Word will also help us to make good choices that will honor God.**

Instructions: Look at the paper. What picture do you see? (a heart with a Bible inside) **This picture will help us to remember that we need to learn God's Word in order to hide it in our hearts.** Have children color the large heart and the Bible inside the heart.

Additional Activities:

- Let children read the passage from a Bible.
- Sing "The B-I-B-L-E" (LOSP 48) and "I Open My Bible Book and Read" (LOSP 54)

I have hidden Your word in my heart.

Psalm 119:11a

Hebrews 12:2a
Let us fix our eyes on Jesus.

To talk about: What does it mean to fix your eyes on something? (stare at it, really focus on it) **I would like everyone to fix their eyes on me right now. That is good everyone is looking at me and paying attention. Let's fix our eyes on something else now.** Pick an object in the room for children to look at. **According to the verse, who are we supposed to fix our eyes on?** (Jesus) **How do we fix our eyes on Jesus since we can't physically see him?** (We think about Jesus and what He wants us to do) **We do that when we come to church or Sunday School, when we read the Bible or pray, anytime we think about Jesus we are fixing our eyes on Him. Why do we want to fix our eyes on Jesus?** (He loved us so much that He died on the cross for us to take away all our sins. He loved us so much that now we want to be like Him by loving others.) **We want to remember all the good things Jesus has done for us. He takes care of us everyday and we want to thank Him for all those things. We also want to pay attention to all Jesus has to teach us so we live our lives so others learn to love Jesus too.**

Instructions: Have children draw a face on the student page. Demonstrate if needed. Put a sticker of Jesus at the top of the page. **So we can remember to fix our eyes on Jesus we're going to draw arrows from the eyes on the people we drew up to Jesus.** Demonstrate how to do this and then help children as needed to draw arrows from the eyes up to the face to Jesus.

Additional activity:

- If you have not already done so, hang a picture of Jesus in your classroom or in your child's bedroom. Talk again about how special Jesus is. **Whenever you look at the picture, it will help you to fix your eyes on Jesus and remember all that He has done for you. It will also help others to fix their eyes on Jesus.**

Let us fix our eyes on Jesus.

Hebrews 12:2a

Matthew 28:6
He has risen, just as He said.

To talk about: Who is He talking about in this verse? Who has risen? (Jesus) **What does it mean to rise?** (get up)**If children are sitting have them rise. In this verse an angel is talking to some women who came to Jesus tomb. Do you know what a tomb is?** (a place they bury people) Show children what a tomb in Jesus day looked like. It was a cave. **Jesus had been killed on a cross and buried. Now an angel was telling the women that He had risen. What does that mean?** (Jesus had come back to life) **Yes, Jesus didn't stay dead. He came back to life just as He said He would. Why did Jesus have to die on the cross?** (to pay for our sins) **Why did He do that?** (He loved us) **Jesus came back to life to show He had won the victory over our sin. After rising, He could also return to heaven and get it ready for us. Someday we will rise from the dead just as Jesus did and go to live in heaven with Him.**

Instructions: There are many symbols that represent new life. Today on our paper what picture do you see? (butterfly) **Caterpillars go into a cocoon** (show a picture if possible) **and they look dead. After a few days, a butterfly bursts from the cocoon. Jesus looked dead, but He burst from the tomb, alive. We're going to color the butterfly and then we'll put a sticker of Jesus on the paper so we can remember, "He is risen, just as He said." Someday Jesus will bring us back to life too.**

Additional Activities:

- Read the crucifixion and resurrection accounts from a Children's Bible.
- Sing songs about Jesus being risen like, "Jesus Christ Is Risen Today" (LOSP p.96) or "Do You Know Who Died For Me" (LOSP p.93)
- Make stained glass butterflies using the pattern from the student page or any pattern you choose. Give each child two butterflies. Have him/her cut the spaces from the inside of the butterflies . Depending on the age of the child, you may have to have the spaces already cut. Glue bright tissue paper squares to the holes on one butterfly. Paste the other butterfly to the first. Display the butterflies in a window or hang them from the ceiling.

He has risen, just as He said.

Matthew 28:6

Psalm 32:10b
The Lord's unfailing love surrounds
the man who trusts in him.

To talk about: Who is the Lord? (God or Jesus) **The verse says God has unfailing love. Do you know what unfailing means?** (It means it will never go away.) **Jesus love is perfect. Jesus' love will always be with you. He will never stop loving you no matter what!** Think of something that children are unlikely to be able to do like to tie their shoes. Ask students to do this task. **How many of you failed to tie your shoes? We are promised that God's love will never fail. He will always show us love. How does God show His unfailing love to you?** (He gives parents, families, food, clothes, house, teachers, friends.) **Most importantly God sent Jesus to die and come back to life to take away all our sins. Do you remember what sins are?** (The bad things we do, say or think) **The verse says the Lord's love surrounds people. What does the word surrounds mean?** (Goes all the way around) **The verse tells us that God's unfailing love surrounds those who trust in God. How do we know if someone trusts in God?** (he/she believes in Jesus) **Does God's love surround you?**

Instructions: Children should put a picture of themselves in the center of the student page. They could also draw a picture of themselves. **Who did we say loves us?** (Jesus, the Lord) **To remember that Jesus loves us we'll put a sticker of Jesus right above our picture. What did we say surrounds means?**(to go all the way around) **What surrounds us?** (God's love) **To show that the Lord's love surrounds you, you're going to make a circle of hearts to go around the picture you put on of yourself. Why would we put hearts in the circle?** (they remind us of love)

Additional activities:

- Sing "Jesus Loves Me" (LOSP 42)
- Say a prayer thanking God for His unfailing love.
- Play this game: Put one child in the center of a circle. Talk about him/her being surrounded. Walk around the child and sing this song to the tune of "Here We Go Round the Mulberry Bush." Jesus love surrounds (insert name of child), surrounds _____, surrounds _____,Jesus love surrounds _____, all of the time.

**The Lord's unfailing love surrounds
the man who trusts in him.**

Psalm 32:10b

Luke 2:11

Today...a Savior has been born to you.

To talk about: God, in this verse, sent an angel to bring good news to a group of shepherds. What did the angel tell the shepherds? (a Savior has been born to you) **Who was the Savior the angel was talking about?** (Jesus) **Do you know what a savior is?** (someone who rescues a person from harm or danger) **For instance, if you were standing on a chair and all of sudden started to fall off, would you be in danger? If I caught you before you could fall and get hurt, I would be your savior. Jesus rescued us from something much bigger than falling off a chair. Not only did He rescue you and me, but He rescued the whole world. Do you know what Jesus rescued us from?** (sin and death) **That is why it was such good news that a Savior has been born to us. He was going to save us from all our sin.**

Instructions: What picture do you see on this paper? (baby Jesus) **Do you know what the bed is called that Jesus is sleeping in?** (a manger) **Do you know what a manger was used for?** (the animals to eat from) **When the angels came to the shepherds, what did they tell them?** (a Savior has been born to you) **Does this little baby sleeping in a manger look like much of a savior?** (no) **Why do you think baby Jesus is sleeping below a big cross? One day Jesus would grow up and die on a cross to save us from our sin. He is our Savior. Who did this baby grow up to be?** (Jesus) **What did Jesus do for us?** (He saved us from our sin) **How did He do that?** (He died on the cross) **Jesus started out as the little baby in the manger. He grew until He became an adult. Then, because He was true God, He died on the cross to take away all our sins. Now God will forgive our sins and not punish us. Let's put a sticker of Jesus on the cross so we can always remember what our Savior Jesus did for us.** Color the picture of baby Jesus and the cross.

Additional activities:

* Read the Christmas account from a children's Bible.
* Using your favorite angel pattern let children make angels. Have the Bible words written on the bottom of the angel. Ask children, **What did the angel tell the shepherds?**

Today...a Savior has been born to you.

Luke 2:11

2 Corinthians 9:15:

Thanks be to God for his indescribable gift.

To talk about: Can you tell me about a favorite present you have received. Those sound like really nice presents, but God has given you and me an even better present than any of those. It is so wonderful that it is hard to imagine or even describe. That is what indescribable means. It is hard to tell people with words what a wonderful gift we've been given. Does anyone know what the gift is that God has given us? (Jesus, His Son) **How did God give us this gift?** (sent Jesus to earth as a baby) **Jesus came to earth and was born. He grew up and eventually died on a cross to forgive all our sins. Jesus rose from the dead or came back to life again. He is our Savior and someday He will take us to live with Him in heaven. Jesus is the most special gift we will ever receive. God gave us the gift of His own son so we could have forgiveness of sins. That is a great amount of love. We should celebrate that God gave us the indescribable gift of our Savior Jesus every day. Can you tell me two times in the church year when we talk a lot about the gift of Jesus?** (Christmas and Easter) **At Christmas time we remember Jesus coming to earth as a baby, and at Easter time we remember the sacrifice Jesus made for us by giving up His life on the cross.**

Instructions: What do you see on this page? (A beautiful present) Have children decorate the present on the page. **What is the best present we will ever receive?** (Jesus as our Savior) **We want to remember that Jesus is the best most indescribable gift we will ever get. To help us remember that, we are going to put a sticker of Jesus in the center of the present.**

Additional activities:

- Sing your favorite songs about Jesus. Say a prayer thanking God for the special gift of Jesus.
- Cut colorful pieces of wrapping paper. Let children glue on a picture of Jesus and put a bow on the paper so they can remember their indescribable gift of Jesus. You may want to write the memory words on the back as the children tell them to you.
- Wrap a present for each child. Inside each gift put a picture of Jesus with the Bible words attached.

Thanks be to God for his indescribable gift.

2 Corinthians 9:15

Exodus 20:8

Remember the Sabbath day by keeping it holy.

To talk about: This verse is one of the ten commandments. A long time ago when God gave His people the Israelites the ten commandments they called the day they worshiped the Sabbath. Do you know what the Sabbath is? (the day set apart for worshiping God.) **What day do we usually worship on?** (Sunday) **Who do we worship?** (God) **Why do we worship God?** (He sent Jesus to be our savior. He made us. He takes care of us) **The verse tells us to keep the Sabbath day holy. What does holy mean?** (set apart and special for God) **How could we remember Sunday and keep it holy or special for God?** (go to church and Sunday School) **When we go to church we are remembering all the wonderful things God has done for us. It is a special time to thank and praise Him with other people who believe in Jesus too. What do we have to thank and praise God for?** (taking care of us, sending Jesus to forgive our sins, loving us, being with us etc.)

Instructions: Demonstrate to children how to draw a simple church on their papers. Be sure to have children put a cross somewhere on their building so they will easily remember it is a church. **We put crosses on our churches so we remember we worship Jesus the one true God.** Instruct children to then draw some people around their church or cut some pictures of people out of a magazine. **What are the people doing?** (Have them repeat the Bible words.)

Additional activity:

- Set up some chairs and pretend to go to church. Sing some songs like "Our Church Family" (LOSP 11) Talk about why we sing special songs called hymns. Tell them a hymn is a song about God. Say a prayer. Read a Scripture. Let children pretend to light the candles and play the organ. Let someone give a short sermon if he/she wants. Talk about each part of the service and why it is important.

**Remember the Sabbath day
by keeping it holy.**

Exodus 20:8

Acts 22:16:
Be baptized and wash your sins away.

To talk about: Can you tell me what happens at baptism? Many people are baptized when they are babies. Parents bring the baby to the front of the church and the Pastor sprinkles water on him or her and says, "I baptize you in the name of the Father and of the Son and of the Holy Spirit." Sometimes people are older when they get baptized and some are dunked completely under the water. The Pastor still says the same words no matter what age a person is baptized. Do you know what happens to the person at baptism? (A person becomes part of God's family and receives faith and forgiveness of sins from God) **The verse says to wash your sins away. Why do we wash things?** (to make them clean) **Our sins make us dirty. What is sin?** (the bad things we do, say or think) **God's Word tells us when we are baptized our sins are washed away. We are made clean. Even though God washes us clean in baptism, we still sin, don't we?** (Yes) **When we tell Jesus we are sorry for the bad things we do, what does He do?** (He forgives us.) **When He forgives us He takes our dirty hearts and cleans them up again.** Be sensitive to those children who may not have been baptized. Reassure them that God still forgives them when they ask and that He still loves them very much.

Instructions: On this paper we see a shell and three drops of water. Do you know why there are three drops on the shell. (To remind us we are baptized in the name of the Father, Son and Holy Spirit the three persons of God.) Have children color the shell with the three drops.

Additional activities:
- Give each child a brown, red and white heart. Attach the three hearts together with a paper fastener so that brown is on the bottom and white is on the top. **The brown color reminds us of dirt and how our hearts are dirty with sin.** Have children write the word sin on the brown heart. **The red heart reminds us that Jesus loves us so much He shed His blood and died for us.** Children write Jesus on the red heart. **White reminds us of something clean. Our hearts are clean now because Jesus forgives us in our baptism and whenever we ask Him.** Children write forgiven on the white heart.
- Sing: "I'm Inright, Outright, Upright, Downright Happy All the time"(LOSP 59) "I Was Baptized, Happy Day" (LOSP 97)
- Take children in the church and show them the baptismal font and discuss what happens at a baptism.

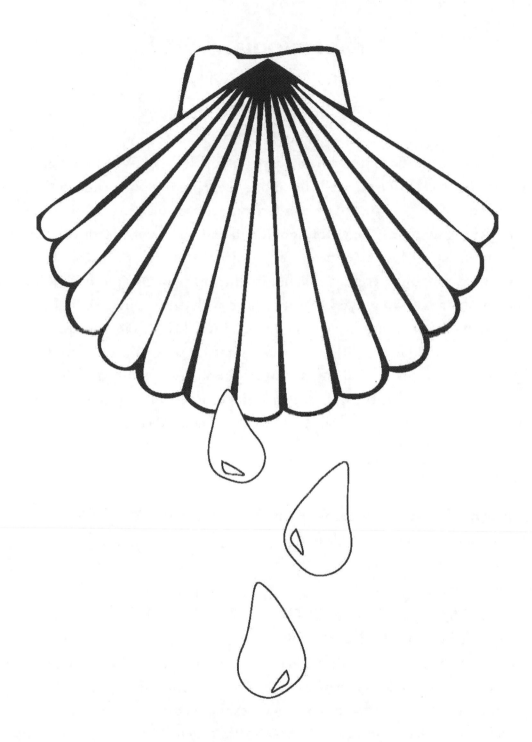

Be baptized and wash your sins away.

Acts 22:16

1 Thessalonians 5:17:
Pray continually.

To talk about: What does it mean to pray? (to talk to God) **What does continually mean?** (all the time) **This verse tells us to pray continually or to talk to God all the time. We can talk to God just like we talk to our moms and dads. He wants us to tell Him everything about our day, both good and bad.** Find some pictures in magazines or old Sunday School leaflets of people engaged in a variety of activities. Discuss the pictures with the children. **Example: What is happening in this picture? What might this person say to God in prayer?** When finished with the pictures ask: **When else can you pray?** (anytime and anywhere) **Why do we pray?** (Jesus is our best friend. He likes when we talk to Him. He helps us and others.) **What are some different kinds of prayer we can say?** (We can thank God) **What can we thank God for?** (sending Jesus to be our Savior, being with us, taking care of us, etc.) **What other kinds of prayer are there?** (We can tell God we are sorry for the bad things we do. That is called confession. We can also ask God to help us and others)

Instructions: Have children draw pictures or cut them from magazines to show places they can pray. Glue magazine pictures on the student page. You could also label the pictures as the children tell you where they can pray.

Additional activities:

- Help children say a prayer. Before beginning, talk about things that have happened during the day. This will help children focus their thoughts. Then let children pray. Each child could say one sentence. If you have a child who is reluctant, you could say a few words and then let him/her repeat you.
- Read a book about prayer: Some good examples are *I Can Pray* by Jennifer Holder and Diane Stortz and *How Did Bible Heros Pray* by Mona Hodgson.

Pray continually.
1 Thessalonians 5:17

Joshua 1:9b
The Lord your God will be with you wherever you go.

To talk about: God promises to be with us always. Where does God live? (some may say in heaven) **Yes, He does live in heaven. Do you know where else God lives?** (in my heart) **Your heart is inside of you and goes everywhere with you; so does Jesus. Can you see God?** (no) **We know God is there because He promises us He will be. God never breaks His promises. He will never leave you. I'd like to share a part of a Bible passage with you. It comes from Psalm 139. It says, "you know when I sit and when I rise." This person is talking to God. He says God knows when I sit. Where are some places you sit? Is God with you when you are sitting? When are some times you rise? Is God with you when you rise? God even knows exactly when you do those things. The Bible also says, "If I go up to the heavens, you are there; if I make my bed in the depths, you are there... If I settle on the far side of the sea, even there your hand will guide me." Can you think of time we might be up in the heavens?** (on an airplane) **Will God be with you on a plane? Have any of you been in the depths like in a cave or underwater? Will God be with you? God is with us no matter where we live and no matter where we go. He will never leave us.**

Instructions: Take a few photos of places that children visit in your town or city or find objects to represent those places. Examples would be a band-aid for a doctor's office or a food label for a grocery store. Talk about each picture or item and ask, **"Is God with you when you go to the doctor?"** (Yes) Have children attach the items or pictures to the student page. Next, have children put a sticker of Jesus above each picture as you discuss them to help children remember that God is with them wherever they go.

Additional activities:

- Take a walk around your school, church, house or outside. Ask: "Is God in our classroom?" Repeat the verse. "Is God with you on the playground?" Repeat the verse. Continue as interest allows.
- Read: *God Lives in My House* by Melody Carlson or your favorite book which talks about God always being with us.

The Lord your God will be with you wherever you go.

Joshua 1:9b

Psalm 13:6
I will sing to the Lord, for He has been good to me.

To talk about: Why do we sing to the Lord? (to thank Him, to tell Him we love Him, to praise Him and to tell Him how great He is) **How has God been good to you?** (He gives food, parents, family, house, clothes, church, etc.) **The best thing God gave us was when He sent His son Jesus to die on the cross for us to take away all our sins. Sometimes even if we are unhappy, we can sing a song to God. Once we start remembering how good God is we may begin to feel better.**

Instructions: Have children draw a face on the student page. Show them how to draw an open mouth to represent singing. They can make a speech balloon and you could add a phrase of a song like, "Jesus loves me this I know." Around the face, children can draw music notes or put stickers of music notes.

Additional activity:

- Sing praises like, "Praise Him Praise Him All You Little Children" (LOSP 68) and "Jesus Loves the Little Children" (LOSP 94) These are only examples. Any song about Jesus you know would be appropriate to sing.

**I will sing to the Lord, for He
has been good to me.**

Psalm 13:6

Galations 3:11b:
The righteous will live by faith.

To talk about: The word righteous means that a person has no guilt or sin. Can anyone be righteous?(no) **The verse says the righteous will live by faith. Who then are the righteous?** (Those who believe in Jesus) **What did Jesus do for us?** (died on the cross to take away all our sins) **Remember righteous means without sin. No person without believing in Jesus can ever be righteous. A person can only be without sin if they believe that Jesus has taken it all away by dying on the cross. Once Jesus forgives us, He no longer sees our sins. Can we be called righteous?** (yes) **The verse says the righteous live by faith. What does it mean to live by faith?** (Trust in Jesus to keep loving us and taking care of us even though we can't see Him.) **We have to trust that God knows best and will always love us even when sad or bad things happen. Asking God to help us and knowing He loves us no matter what is how we live by faith. Who gives us our faith?**(God) **When did He do that?** (When we were baptized or when we heard His Word) **How can we keep our faith strong?** (Keep listening to and reading His word; praying)

Instructions: Have children draw a picture of themselves at the bottom of the student page and then put a sticker of Jesus at the top of the page. Tape a cloud shape over Jesus so the cloud can be lifted to reveal Jesus any time the children want to. **Can you still see Jesus under the cloud?** (no) **Do we know that Jesus is still there?** (Yes) **That is what faith is. We keep believing in Jesus even thought we can't see Him with our eyes.**

Additional Activities:

- If children are willing, blindfold them and lead them around the room. Ask: **"Did you trust me not to let you bump into anything? You trusted me even though you couldn't see me. That is just like our faith in Jesus. Even though we can not see Him we trust in Him to love and forgive us. Jesus promises that He will always love us and Jesus always keeps His promises."**
- Make a wall hanging for your classroom or your child's room. Hang a picture of Jesus and then have children work together to make a mosaic with torn construction paper pieces. Ask the children to say the Bible words. Write them on the mosaic, and then hang the mosaic over the picture of Jesus. Talk again about even though Jesus can't be seen, He is still with us. Lift the mosaic to demonstrate.

The righteous will live by faith.

Galations 3:11b

Psalm 134:2:
Lift up your hands in the sanctuary and praise the Lord.

To talk about: Everyone lift up your hands. How can lifting our hands be a way of praising God? (It could draw our attention up to God) **Do you know what a sanctuary is?** (a church) **A sanctuary is also considered a safe place. Why is that a fitting name for a church?** (We are always safe in God's care.) **How do we praise God in our sanctuary?** (sing, pray, listen to God's Word) **Where else can we praise God?** (anywhere and everywhere) **Why do we want to praise God?** (He loves us so much He sent Jesus to be our Savior and forgive our sins. He is always with us and cares for us.)

Instructions: Can you tell me what you see in the picture? (Hands and a cross) **Which way are the hands pointing?** (up) **Everyone lift up your hands. When we lift our hands up, our hands are above our arms. All these hands are lifted up. One way people praise the Lord is to lift their hands. Notice also some of the hands are big and some of them are smaller. It doesn't matter what age you are. Everyone can praise the Lord. What does the cross remind us of?** (Jesus) **Where do we often go when we worship Jesus.** (church) **Can you remember another word for church from our Bible words?** (sanctuary) **People don't always raise their hands to praise the Lord, but it is one way to praise Him. The important thing to remember is that whenever we go to worship, we praise God in our sanctuary in many different ways.** Have children color the picture on the student page.

Additional activity:

- Lead children in a litany of praise. A litany is a prayer where a leader recites the petitions alternately with the people who generally have a fixed response.

  > **Leader: Dear God, Thank you for our church.**
  > Children: Praise the Lord! (let them lift up their hands and wave them when they say these words.)
  > **Leader: Thank you for our pastor.**
  > Children: Praise the Lord!
  > Additional thoughts for the leader: Thank you for our school, our family, food, clothes, home, our Savior Jesus.

Lift up your hands in the sanctuary and praise the Lord.

Psalm 134:2

Philippians 3:20a

Our citizenship is in heaven.

To talk about: Do you know what a citizen is? (a person who lives in a certain town or country, a person who is also able to enjoy certain privileges like voting because they live there) **What town are you a citizen of? What state? What country? This Bible verse tells us our real home is in heaven. God gives us homes on earth, but someday we will live forever in heaven with Jesus. We will be a citizen of heaven. Who will live in heaven?** (Everyone who believes in Jesus as their Savior) **What did Jesus save us from?** (our sins) **What are our sins?** (The bad things we do, say, or think) **What will heaven be like?** (Happy place, no crying or fighting, bright because we'll be surrounded by God's light.)

Instructions: Have children draw a cloud shape at the top of the student page. Have children color it yellow and orange to represent the happiness and brightness of heaven. **Who lives in heaven?** (Jesus) **We'll put a sticker of Jesus in the cloud to help us remember that Jesus lives in heaven and some day we will live there too.** Have children draw a picture of themselves at the bottom of the page. Draw an arrow from the picture of them up to heaven. **Right now your home is on earth, but the arrow shows that one day you will live in heaven with Jesus.**

Additional activity:

- Discuss the physical place of heaven and make a class mural or students can make individual pictures. Write the Bible words at the top or bottom. Tell the children that while we never know exactly what heaven will be like until we get there, God, in the Bible, has given us some clues to help us imagine heaven. Read the following verses so children know what to include in their pictures. The pictures can either be drawn or patterns and other pictures can be provided. Read Revelation 5:11 - lots of angels, Revelation 7:9-10 - lots of people from every nation, God on a throne, Jesus, Revelation 21:4 - everyone is happy, Revelation 21:21 - streets of pure gold

Our citizenship is in heaven.

Philippians 3:20a

Psalm 139:14a

I praise you because I am fearfully
and wonderfully made.

To talk about: God made you special. Each body part is put just where He wants it to be. God gives you special ideas and hobbies. No one is just like you! Suggest some things you think are special about the children. Example: God made you a good singer. Do you know what the word fearfully means? (Children may answer that it is scary) **Sometimes fearfully does mean scary, but fearfully can also have another meaning. In this verse, it means awesome. It is another word for wonderful. We say, "Wow God, I am amazing. All my parts work together and you have given me special interests. Nobody is just like me. You are awesome.** Ask children to make suggestions as to what they think is special about them.

Instructions: Find or take pictures of children involved in activities they enjoy. Glue several on the student page. If actual photographs are unavailable, have children draw things they like to do. As you talk about the pictures with children, remind them that you are thankful that God has made them just as they are.

Additional activities:

- Let children look in a mirror. Talk about their physical characteristics or body parts. Example: God gave you brown hair and blue eyes.
- Let children make thumb prints. Talk about how every person's thumb print is different. Talk about how great God is to make every person different.

I praise you because I am fearfully and wonderfully made.

Psalm 139:14a

1Corinthians 10:31

So whether you eat or drink or whatever
you do, do it all for the glory of God.

To talk about: What does do it all for the glory of God mean? (do everything to please God) **The word glory means giving high honor or distinction. Everything we do should not only please God, but should be done in such a way that He is honored. How can we please God when we eat and drink?** (pray, use manners, be kind to family members) **How can we please God when we...?** Fill in the blank here. Examples include: when we ride in the car, when we play with friends, when we come to school. **When should we please God?** (all the time) **Why do we want to please God?** (because we love Him and because He loves us and has done so much for us.) **We also want others to come to know and love God like we do. When we do things to honor God, His name is spread to all those we come in contact with. What has God done for us?** (He sent Jesus to be our Savior and to forgive us all our sins.) **God loves us so much and so we want to do all we can to please Him and to show love to others. That brings God glory.**

Instructions: Look at the top of our paper. What do you see? (a family eating together) **Which part of the verse does that remind you of?** (whether you eat or drink) Have children color the family sitting down to a meal. **The verse also says whatever you do. What does that mean?** (everything I do should be done in a manner that pleases God) Find some photos of the child engaged in different activities and help him/her glue them on the page. If photos are unavailable, children could draw a couple of pictures showing them doing things they enjoy. They could also find pictures in magazines.

Additional activity:

- Take your class or your child on a picnic. A special snack time would work just as well as a meal. If the weather is questionable, spread a blanket on the floor. Talk about eating and drinking and bringing glory to God. Enjoy the class or family experience.

So whether you eat or drink

**or whatever you do,
do it all for the glory of God.**

1 Corinthians 10:31

Matthew 4:19

"Come follow Me," Jesus said, "and I
will make you fishers of men."

To talk about: What does it mean to follow Jesus? (When we believe in Jesus and that He died and rose again to save us, we want to do the things Jesus wants us to do.) **Jesus in this verse is talking to some men who were fishermen. What do you think they were fishing for?** (fish) **Jesus wanted these men to be His disciples and travel with Him. He told them He would make them fishers of men. Do you think Jesus meant to hook people with a net or a fishing line to catch them?** (no) **What did Jesus mean when He said He would make them fishers of men?** (He would help them learn how to tell others about God and the promised Savior) **Can we be a fisher of men?** (Yes) **We can tell others about Jesus. We can also do kind things for others like Jesus would do. Who does Jesus want us to be a fisher to?** (Everyone)

Instructions: Above the word follow on the student page, have children draw three vertical lines. Have them attach a circle on top. Tell students, **"These lines and circles are going to be people. They look like they are playing follow the leader."** Place a sticker of Jesus above the word Jesus. **This sticker will remind us that Jesus is talking? What did Jesus say?** (come follow me, I will make you fishers of men) Place a picture of the child above the word you, or have them draw a picture of themselves. **Jesus wants you to be a fisher of men. He wants you to tell people how much Jesus loves them.** Show children how to draw a simple fish and have them draw a picture of a fish above the word fish. Next, have children cut pictures of people out of magazines to represent the men. **All these people remind us that Jesus wants all people to know about Him.**

Additional activities:

- Play Follow the Leader. Remind children their leader every day is Jesus. Just like we copy the leader in the game, we want to copy Jesus' actions because we love Him and are so happy He took away all our sins.
- Set up a pond with paper fish. On one side glue a picture of a person. Put a large paper clip on each fish. Let children go fishing for men with a stick or pole that has a magnet attached to it. When they catch a fish, help them to practice saying words to the person on their fish like, "Jesus loves you. Jesus takes away all your sins. Jesus is with you."

"Come follow Me," Jesus said,

and I will make you fishers

of men.

Matthew 4:19

Proverbs 18:10

The name of the Lord is a strong tower;
the righteous run to it and are safe.

To talk about: If possible show a picture of a castle. **Find the towers. How would this tower help keep people safe?** (It is big and strong) **Look at how thick and strong the walls are. It would take a lot of fighting to break down the wall? Our verse says the name of the Lord is a strong tower. Remember God is stronger than the thickest tallest castle wall. The verse says the righteous run to God and are safe. Who are the righteous?** (anyone who believes in Jesus as their Savior, that He died and came back to life.) **Do you believe in Jesus? Are you righteous? How do we run to the Lord or to God?** (Pray) **Anytime we talk to God we are running to God. He helps and protects us just like the strong tower on the castle.**

Instructions: What picture is on our paper? (a tower) Have children trace over the word Lord with their finger. **Does anyone know what the word on the tower says?** (Lord) **Remember Lord is another name for God.** Have children color and decorate the tower on the page.

Additional activity:

- Let children build towers out of blocks. Then let them run to the towers and repeat the Bible words.

The name of the Lord is a strong tower;

the righteous run to it and are safe.

Proverbs 18:10

Matthew 7:14:

Small is the gate and narrow the road that leads to life.

To talk about: Do you know what narrow means? (not very wide) Show children a narrow place or show them how to demonstrate wide and narrow using their hands. **The verse says the narrow road leads to life. What is the life this verse is talking about?** (eternal life in heaven) **What do we know about heaven?** (It is a wonderful, happy place) **How does a person get to heaven?** (By believing Jesus died on the cross and came back to life) **Why did Jesus die on the cross?** (To forgive all our sins) **Is there any other way to get to heaven?** (no) **That is why this verse says small is the gate and narrow is the road because the only way anyone will get into heaven is if they believe Jesus is their Savior. Many people think that if they are a good person they will go to heaven. Some people think it doesn't matter which God you believe in that they are all the same so everyone will go to heaven. This verse reminds us that there is only one way to heaven and that is believing that Jesus died for them.**

Instructions: Have children draw a narrow road with their pencils on the student page. Put a sticker of Jesus at the top of the road. Draw yellow and orange lines all around Jesus. These colors represent the bright and happy place of heaven. Make a small gate out of construction paper. Glue one side of the gate down so the gate can open and shut. Have children draw a picture of themselves on the road.

Additional activities:

- Sing happy songs about Jesus such as, "Let Us Sing For Joy" (LOSP p.105)
- Allow children to walk on a balance beam. Older children could try the balance beam using the wide side of the board and then the narrow side. **Which is easier to walk on the wide side or the narrow side?** If using only one side, **Is it hard to stay on a narrow board? It is hard to walk on something narrow without falling off. We need God's help so that we stay on the narrow road to heaven.** Help each child say a simple prayer asking God to help them stay on the narrow path. **Dear God, I believe in Jesus. I believe He died to take all my sins away. Please help me to stay on the narrow road so that someday I can live in heaven with you. Amen.**

**Small is the gate and narrow
the road that leads to life.**

Matthew 7:14

Philippians 4:4:

Rejoice in the Lord always. I will say it again: Rejoice!

To talk about: What does rejoice mean? (be happy) **How can we be happy in the Lord always?** (remember all God gives us and all we have) **What if we are having a bad or sad day? How can we still rejoice in the Lord?** (Remember God is always with us even when we are sad. Remember Jesus loves and cares for us, and He will never take those things away from us.)

Instructions: Have children draw and color a big happy face on the student page. **Why would we draw a big happy face on our papers?** (to remember to be happy in the Lord.)

Additional activities:

- Sing "Rejoice in the Lord Always" (LOSP 52)
- Make pom-poms using a piece of newspaper or construction paper. Roll the paper up to make a long tube. Tape the tube together toward the bottom. Cut several strips beginning at the top. Cut ½ to ¾ of the way down the tube. Have children wave the pom-poms and chant: Rejoice, Rejoice, Always Rejoice OR Rejoice in the Lord, Rejoice in the Lord, Rejoice in the Lord ALWAYS! Let children make up their own cheers while praising God.

Rejoice in the Lord always. I will say it again: rejoice.

Philippians 4:4

Matthew 5:14a

You are the light of the world.

To talk about: What does a light do? (makes a dark place bright) Demonstrate this using a flashlight if possible. **Jesus is speaking to us in this verse. He is telling us that we are the light of the world. When people know Jesus their lives are brighter and happier. What do you think it means to be the light of the world?** (Jesus wants us to tell others about Him.) He wants us to shine His light to other people so they will believe in Him and to know that He died and rose again from the dead to take away all their sins.) **We shine Jesus love to other people. How can we do that?** (We can talk to people and tell them Jesus loves them.) **People also watch the way we act. If we play nicely with other children and share with them, that is being a light. We are showing other people that we love Jesus. If we talk nicely with people and not say bad things to them or to others that is being a light. Can you think of other ways to be a light? Is it easy to be a light?** (no) **Who can help us be a light?** (Jesus) **We can do anything with Jesus help. He will help us tell others and be His shining light.**

Instructions: Children should place a picture of themselves over the word you on the student page. Have them paste a square of yellow construction paper over the word light. **This yellow paper reminds me of the sun and how it lights up the world. We are to light up the world too by telling others about Jesus.** Have children put a sticker of the world over the word world.

Additional activities:

- Sing "This Little Gospel Light of Mine" (LOSP 103)
- Have children make cards to send or give to someone they want to share Jesus with.

You

are the light

of the world.
Matthew 5:14a

1 Corinthians 12:18

God has arranged the parts in the body, every one of them, just as He wanted them to be.

To talk about: Do you know what arranged means? (put in a certain place) Demonstrate the word arrange with some blocks or even with arranging the children in a line. **The verse is telling us that God arranged or put every part of our body right where it would work the best. Ask questions like, "What would we do if our feet were by our ears? How would we walk?" Isn't it wonderful how God made us! Our bodies are amazing. Besides our physical body, God has also given us another body. All people who believe in Jesus are called the body of Christ. Once again He puts us all together for a special reason. Everyone has different things he or she is good at. God arranges us all together in a certain way so we can serve Him better.**

Instructions: Have children draw a picture of a person on the student page. You may want to draw one part of a person at at time on a white board and have the children copy you. This will help them learn all the body parts. Talk about each part as you draw it. Remind children to include any parts they may forget to draw if they are doing the project independently.

Additional activities:

- Sing songs about different body parts like "I Can Stamp"(LOSP 21) or "I Have Hands That Can Clap"(LOSP 29)
- On a piece of cardboard, draw a person. Cut it apart like a puzzle. Have children arrange the parts to make a person. You could have each child make their own puzzle. Talk again about how wonderfully God made our bodies with all our parts arranged perfectly.

God has arranged the parts in the body, every one of them, just as He wanted them to be.

1 Corinthians 12:18

Psalm 118:24

This is the day the Lord has made; let
us rejoice and be glad in it.

To talk about it: God makes and gives us every new day. What does rejoice mean?
(be happy and thankful) **How can we rejoice and be glad for the day God has made?**
(We can think about all the things we have to be thankful for and say a prayer thanking
God for them. We can thank Him for all the special events that will happen. We can sing
songs that talk about how wonderful Jesus is.) **Everyday when we get up we only need
to look out the window. We can rejoice at all the things we see that God has made
like the sun, the trees, the grass, our families, and our pets. When we see all these
things, we can't help but remember how wonderful our God is. We have to rejoice
and be glad in the day that God has made for us. We can also be reminded that God
is everywhere especially right with us. Sometimes the day may be rather sad. Is that
still a day God has made?** (Yes) **We can always rejoice that God loves us even when
we are sad.**

Instructions: Let children draw a picture of the day or let them find pictures of people in
magazines engaged in daytime activities and paste them on the student page. Put a large
happy face sticker or draw a happy face at the top of the paper. **What does the happy
face remind us of?** (rejoice or be happy with the day God has given us.)

Additional activities:

- Sing: "This is the Day" (LOSP 53)
- Let children list things they can rejoice in today. If no one mentions it, be sure
  to include that knowing Jesus loves and forgives us is something we can rejoice
  and be glad in every day. Use children's responses to say a responsive prayer.
  Leader says: **Dear God, Thank you for _____. This is the
  day the Lord has made.** Children say: Let us rejoice and be glad in it.

This is the day the Lord has made;
Let us rejoice and be glad in it.

Psalm 118:24

Psalm 18:2b

My God is my rock, in whom I take refuge.

To talk about: In this verse, what do we call God? (a rock) **Why do you think we call God our Rock?** (He is strong like a rock. He is so strong and powerful He is in control of everything.) **Do you know what a refuge is?** (a safe place to go, somewhere we can go where we won't be hurt) **Can you think of some places that might be thought of as a refuge?** (school, home, church) **Why do you think we might say we take refuge in God?** (We know He loves us. We know he will comfort us and help us.) **God will never reject us. We can count on God always. That is why He is our refuge. How can we take refuge in God?** (pray) **We take refuge in God whenever we talk to Him. He will listen to all our thoughts even if we are sad, angry or afraid. He loves us no matter what and wants to help us. He hears and answers our prayers.**

Instructions: What is on our paper today? (a rock) **"What does the word in the middle say?"** (God) **God is our rock. He is always strong even in times of trouble. We know He will always be there for us.** Color the huge rock.

Additional activities:

- Sing: "My God is So Great, So Strong and So Mighty"(LOSP 64)
- Find big rocks and let the children decorate with markers. Write the word God on the rock. Tell children that whenever they look at their rock, they should remember God and how strong He is. They can talk to Him anytime and anywhere, and He will be their refuge.

**My God is my rock, in
whom I take refuge.**

Psalm 18:2b

Psalm 56:3

When I am afraid, I will trust in you.

To talk about: What are some things that make you afraid? Sometimes there are things that frighten us. This verse tells us what to do when we are afraid. It says, "I will trust in you."Who is you talking about in the verse? (God) **Whom are we to trust when we are afraid?** (God) **The Bible verse says that when we're afraid we should trust in God. When we are afraid, what are some things we can remember about God?** (He is always with us. We can talk to Him and He will hear us. He loves us. He takes care of us.)

Instructions: Look at the girl on this paper. How does she look? (afraid) **Her eyes look like there is something that is scaring her, don't they? What is she doing with her hands?** (praying) **When we pray we are trusting in Jesus. Our verse says, "When I am afraid I will trust in you." Let's put a sticker of Jesus above the girl to show that she is trusting in Jesus.** Have children color the picture.

Additional activities:

- Make up a simple song with the children. Examples: (Tune: "Mary Had A Little Lamb") When I am afraid of the dark, afraid of the dark, afraid of the dark, When I am afraid of the dark, I will trust in You. Substitute other fears listed in the talk about section or insert common childhood fears. (Tune:"Are You Sleeping") When I am afraid, When I am afraid, I will trust, I will trust, I will trust in you God. I will trust in you God. Yes I will. Yes I will.

- **We can also say a prayer to God asking Him to help us trust in Him when we feel afraid.** Using some of the fears listed in the talk about section, help children say a litany. As an example: Leader: **When a storm comes,** Children: Help us to trust in you. Leader: **When I get sick,** Children: Help us to trust in you.

When I am afraid, I will trust in you.

Psalm 56:3

Isaiah 64:8

We are the clay, you are the potter; we
are all the work of your hand.

To talk about: If possible, show children a picture or program of a potter at work and some of his/her finished products. **Potters throw a lump of wet clay on a spinning wheel and then work the clay with their hands until they make a vase or bowl or some other object. Isn't it amazing how potters can take a lump of clay and make it into something beautiful. This verse tells us we are like the clay, and God is the potter. Did He throw us on a spinning wheel and shape us?** (no)**He made each one of us special and unique. The great thing is that just like the potter continues to work the clay until it is just right, God continues to make us more and more beautiful each day. He knows what He wants us to look like so he keeps shaping us our whole life. He helps us to continue to grow in our faith. He helps us to learn to help others and tell others about Him.**

Instructions: Have children make a large cloud at the top of their student page. Next, help them trace their fingers placed tightly together so it looks like a hand coming out of the cloud. **This is a symbol to help us remember God our Father in heaven is our potter and He made us.** Next, have children draw a picture of themselves under the hand. **Didn't God make you beautiful?**

Additional activity:

- Make your favorite clay recipe or get out the play dough. Let children be potters. Thank God for making us all beautiful.

We are the clay, you are the potter,
we are all the work of your hand

Isaiah 64:8

Acts 3:19

Repent and turn to God, so that
your sins may be wiped out.

To talk about: Do you know what the word repent means? (to tell God we are sorry for our sins and to ask God to help us not do that sin any more) **How do we do that?** (by praying) **We might say, "Dear Jesus, I am sorry for fighting with my brother. Please forgive me and help me to be nice to him. Amen. That is called confessing our sins. When we pray, we turn to God. What does this verse say will happen to our sins when we repent?** (God will wipe them out.) **He will forgive us and will not even remember our sins anymore. Why does He do that?** (He loves us.)

Instructions: What is the picture on our paper? (praying hands) **Today we talked about a special kind of prayer called confession. Do you remember what we do in that prayer?** (Repent, or say we are sorry for doing something bad.) **These hands are going to remind us to repent and turn to God in prayer.** Children can color the hands if they desire. Over the word sins, have them draw a box and color it black. Ask: **Why would I have you color the box black?** (Our sins make us dirty and ugly) Over the words wiped out, have children draw a box and leave it white. Ask: **What happened to our dirty sins?** (They are gone) **When we ask Jesus to forgive us, He completely gets rid of all our sins. He wipes them out so they do not make us dirty any more.**

Additional activities:

- Talk about some of the sins children frequently commit. Have them draw a sin they commit on a white board. Help them say a prayer of repentance and then let them wipe out their sin. Remind them that Jesus has done that with their sin. He has completely forgiven them and forgotten their sin. Jesus has wiped their sin out.
- Sing: "I Am Sorry Jesus" (LOSP p.14)

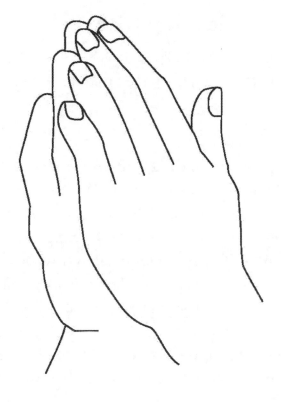

Repent and turn to God

so that your sins may

be wiped out.

Acts 3:19

Matthew 28:19b

baptizing them in the name of the Father,
and of the Son, and of the Holy Spirit.

To talk about: When a person is baptized God the Father gives a him or her faith and sends God the Holy Spirit to live within them. Whenever someone is baptized the Pastor says these words, "I baptize you in the name of the Father, and of the Son, and of the Holy Spirit." Who is the Father, Son and Holy Spirit? (God) **We call the three different persons of God the Trinity. Trinity means three in one. Who are the three persons of the Trinity?** (Father, Son and Holy Spirit) **Each person of God has a special job but they are still one God. God our Father created us and He controls everything that happens in the world. God the Son is Jesus. He died on the cross for us. He is our Savior. God the Holy Spirit gives us faith and helps us to live for God.** You could also demonstrate the Trinity using an apple or an egg. The apple has three parts the core, the flesh and the peel. The egg also has three parts the yolk, the whites, and the shell.

Instructions: What shape is on our paper? (triangle) **How many sides does a triangle have?** (three) **This triangle is going to be our symbol for the Trinity, our three-in-one God. There is one shape with three separate sides.** Talk about the symbols for the Father, Son and Holy Spirit found on the corners of the triangle. **The hand reminds us of God the Father and that He made us. The picture of Jesus shows God the Son our Savior. The dove shows God the Holy Spirit. They are all connected on the one triangle. We have one God with three different persons.** Have children color the triangle.

Additional activities:

- Read the account of Jesus baptism from a children's Bible or from the Bible (John 1:29-34) Be sure to point out all the persons of the Trinity present at the baptism. God the Son is being baptized, God the Father calls from heaven and God the Holy Spirit descends like a dove.
- Let the children make a symbol of the trinity to decorate with markers, glitter or beads. Some suggestions include a triangle, three circles connected or a shamrock. Have children tell you the three persons of the Trinity.
- Read the book *3 in 1 (A Picture Book of God)* by Joanne Marxhausen.

Baptizing them in the name of the Father, and of the Son and of the Holy Spirit.

Matthew 28:19

Isaiah 43:1b:

I have summoned you by name, you are mine.

To talk about: Pick a student and ask them to come to you. **Do you know what I just did?** (Called someone to the front) **Another word for calling is summoned. We could say I called you or I summoned you. How might you summon your dog? Do you know who is speaking in this verse?** (God) **Who has called you and knows your name?** (God) **Can you actually hear God call you like you can hear me talking to you?** (no) **When did God first call you?** (at baptism or as you hear His Word in the Bible and begin to understand it) **This verse tells us that God knows our name and that we belong to Him. What does it mean to belong to God?** (It means He will always love us, take care of us, be with us, teach us and forgive us for all the bad things we do.) **Isn't it wonderful to belong to God! He will never ever forget us. He will always know right where we are, and He knows our name.**

Instructions: Today, we are going to put a sticker of Jesus in the middle of our paper. Remember that Jesus is God's Son and that He is God. We use a picture of Jesus, God's son because we don't have a picture of God our Father. No one has ever seen Him. Have children place a sticker or a large picture of Jesus in the center of the page. Show them how to draw a speech bubble coming from Jesus mouth. **This bubble shows that Jesus is saying something. What do you think He would say? He is summoning you by name. Please write your name in the speech bubble.**

Additional activity:

- Trace stencils or draw balloon letters for each child's name. Let them decorate using whatever method you prefer. Place them around a picture of Jesus. Include the Bible Words somewhere in your display.

**I have summoned you by
name, you are mine.**

Isaiah 43:1b

Revelation 19:16b
King of Kings and Lord of Lords.

To talk about: What does a king do? (He rules over and leads people under his care. It is also his job to take care of the people in his kingdom) If possible show children a picture of a king. **Who do you think this verse is talking about when it says King of Kings and Lord of Lords?** (Jesus) **When the Bible says Jesus is King of Kings what does that mean?** (It means Jesus is more powerful and greater than any other king on earth. He is the best King ever) **Where is His kingdom?** (all of earth and all of heaven) **Whose king is Jesus?** (He is our King. He leads and guides us and takes care of us.) **What does Lord of Lords mean?** (It means Jesus is true God) **Even though people may worship other gods, Jesus is the strongest and most powerful God. Only our God is alive and real. Only our God can forgive our sins. Only our God shows love to people and takes care of them. There is no one like Jesus and the Bible tells us that someday every knee will bow at Jesus name. Every person on earth will have to admit that Jesus truly is the best king and the only God.**

Instructions: Have children place a picture of Jesus in the center of the page. Let them draw and color a crown above the picture of Jesus, or have crowns already cut from construction paper that children can glue above Jesus.

Additional activities:

- Sing "He is King of Kings"
- Let children make cardboard crowns to wear. Let them decorate with jewels if desired. In the center, place a sticker of Jesus. On the bottom write: Jesus is my King!

King of Kings and Lord of Lords.

Revelation 19:16b

1 John 1:9

If we confess our sins, he is faithful and just and will forgive our sins.

To talk about: What does confess mean?(to say with our mouth) **What is sin?**(bad things we say, do or think) **This verse tells us we should tell Jesus the bad things we have done. You can say something like, "I'm sorry Jesus for disobeying my mommy," This is called confession. What does God say will happen when we confess our sins?** (He will forgive them.) **What does the word forgive mean?** (He will not remember the bad things we have done. He forgives us because Jesus died for us) **This verse describes Jesus as faithful. Faithful means it is something Jesus will always do. We can count on God to do what He says; and if we are sorry for our sins, He will also be fair or just to forgive us. God keeps His promises to us one hundred percent of the time.**

Instructions: Place a picture of the child or have the child draw himself in the bottom corner of the student page. Draw a speech bubble from the child saying, "I'm sorry Jesus." **When you tell Jesus you are sorry for your sin, what is that called?** (confession) Place a sticker of Jesus in the top corner. Draw a speech bubble from Jesus. **After you confess your sins to Jesus, what will He say to you?** (I forgive you.) Write, "I forgive you, _____ name _____." inside the the speech balloon coming from Jesus.

Additional activity:

- Have children talk about some sins they have done. Hand out a picture of a cross. Inside the cross have them draw pictures of sins they have committed. Help them to say a simple prayer asking Jesus to forgive them. When finished, glue an identical cross shape over the top of their sins to show Jesus has forgiven and forgotten the sins they have done. **What happened to your sins?** (Jesus took them away forever by His death on the cross.) Help them say a simple prayer thanking Jesus for being faithful and just and forgiving them all their sin.

If we confess our sins, he is faithful and just and will forgive our sins.

1 John 1:9

Romans 10:15b:

How beautiful are the feet of those who bring good news.

To talk about: What is the good news this verse is talking about? (Jesus loved us so much He died on the cross to save us all from our sin so someday we can live in heaven with Him.) **Whose feet are beautiful?** (those who tell others about Jesus) **God in this passage is not saying that just a person's feet are beautiful, but anyone who tells others about Jesus. Who are some people who tell you about Jesus?** (pastor, parents, siblings, friends, teachers) **Can you tell others about Jesus?** (Yes) **What are some things you can say about Jesus?** (Jesus loves you, He died for you, He forgives you, He is with you) **Why would God say that people who tell others about Him are beautiful?** (He wants everyone in the world to know about Him. He uses people to get His message out to others.)

Instructions: Do you know who is in this picture? (a pastor) **What is the pastor holding?** (a bible) **Why would a pastor be holding a Bible?** (The good news about Jesus is in the Bible.) **The pastor's job is to tell everyone about the good news of Jesus from the Bible. Is it only the pastor's job to tell others about Jesus?** (no) **We all should tell others the good news we have heard from the Bible.** Have children color the picture.

Additional activities:

- Let children decorate paper feet so they are beautiful. Hang them on the wall or bulletin board with Jesus in the middle. Put the Bible verse on the board.
- Let children make a poster of people who tell them about Jesus. Have them repeat the Bible words as you write them on their posters.
- Let them make a poster of who they can tell about Jesus.

**How beautiful are the feet of
those who bring good news.**

Romans 10:15b

2 Corinthians 9:7b
God loves a cheerful giver.

To talk about: What does cheerful mean? (happy) **A cheerful giver is someone who gladly shares the things they have with others. We can give God back some of the things He has given us. One thing we can give God is our time. How can we give God our time?** (We can go to church and Sunday School. We can listen to mom or dad read the Bible. We can pray and help others.) **How many of you pick up your toys right away when your mom asks? Are you being a cheerful giver? Another thing we can share is our talent. A talent is something we are good at. Can you think of something you are good at? How can you share your talent? We can also share our treasures. Our treasure is the money or physical goods we have. Have you ever gotten money as a present? Instead of spending all your money on candy or toys, could you happily give some back to Jesus? Why would we want to be a cheerful giver?** (God has given us everything we have. He loves us so much He sent His only Son Jesus to be our Savior. God shares everything with us, so we want to share with others)

Instructions: Do you remember the three things we can share with God and others? (time, talents and treasure.) **What kind of picture would help us to remember to share our time?** (a clock or watch) Show children how to draw a clock. Allow them to draw a clock on their student paper. **Can you think of a way we can remember the word talent? Remember talents are the things we are good at that we can share with other people. Let's trace your hand on the paper to remember a talent is something you do. What did we say our treasure was?** (money). **I'm going to share a penny with you and we will tape it on our papers. What kind of giver does God want us to be?** (cheerful) **Let's put a smiley face sticker at the top of our papers to remind us to be cheerful givers.**

Additional activity:

- Practice being cheerful givers. Visit or sing at a nursing home. Collect items for a needy family in your neighborhood. Do a project around your church like planting flowers. Pray for a missionary family. These are only a small number of examples. Maybe your students have some ideas.

God loves a cheerful giver.

2 Corinthians 9:7b

Jeremiah 29:12b

Come and pray to me, and I will listen to you.

To talk about: Who is talking in this verse? (God) **What is prayer?** (talking to God) **God is telling us that He wants us to talk to Him. What can we talk to God about?** (anything, good, bad, and sad things, when we're afraid, happy, sick or in trouble) **We can also pray for others and talk to God about how happy we are to have Him in our lives. We can thank Him for sending Jesus to take away all our sins. What does God promise will happen when we pray to Him?** (He will listen to us.) **Every time we pray no matter where we are God will listen to us. Even if no one else can hear us, God can and does listen to us.**

Instructions: What do you see on the paper? (a person praying) **Who are we supposed to pray to?** (God) Have children color the picture and place a sticker of Jesus above the picture to show the person is praying to God.

Additional activities:

- Take your children on a walk around your neighborhood, church, or school. Make numerous stops on your walk to pray with the children. It is a prayer walk. Pray for people you know who may be sick, pray for pastors and teachers, thank God for His goodness in sending Jesus. Ask children if they have anything they want to pray for. Remember to talk about that no matter where you have been on your walk, God has gone with you and is listening to your prayers.

- Teach your children about the different kinds of prayer.
    - a. Praise when we tell God how wonderful He is
    - b. Confession when we tell God we are sorry for our sins
    - c. Supplication when we ask God for things for ourselves and others
    - d. Thanksgiving when we tell God thank you for all He has given

- A prayer could be written on a paper so children can fill in the blanks. An example follows. Dear Jesus, I praise you because you are _____. I am sorry for _____. Please help _____. Thank you God for _____. Amen

**Come and pray to me and
I will listen to you.**

Jeremiah 29:12